5106

P9-BIL-742

How to Draw the Life and Times of
John Tyler

Dulce Zamora

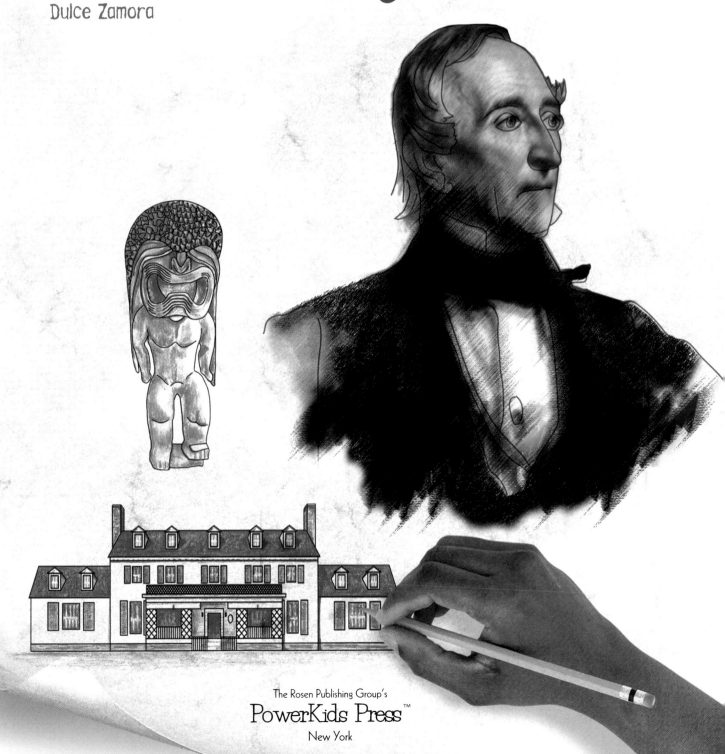

The Rosen Publishing Group's
PowerKids Press™
New York

Here's to my parents, Francisco and Lilia Zamora, for giving me enough heart and backbone to fly

Published in 2006 by The Rosen Publishing Group, Inc.
29 East 21st Street, New York, NY 10010

First Edition

Editor: Rachel O'Connor
Layout Design: Elana Davidian

Illustrations: All illustrations by Holly Cefrey.
Photo Credits: pp. 4, 16 Library of Congress Prints and Photographs Division; pp. 7, 26 (portrait) White House Historical Association (White House Collection) (34, 160); p. 8 (house) © Hulton Archive/Getty Images; p. 9 © Benton J. Nelson, www.presidentsgraves.com; pp. 10, 22, 24 (map) © North Wind Picture Archives; p. 12 © Corbis; p. 14 © Richard T. Nowitz/Corbis; p. 18 Picture History; pp. 20, 28 © Bettmann/Corbis; p. 24 (flag) © Richard Cummins/Corbis; p. 26 (house) © Lee Snider/Photo Images/Corbis.

Library of Congress Cataloging-in-Publication Data

Zamora, Dulce.
How to draw the life and times of John Tyler / Dulce Zamora.— 1st ed.
    p. cm. — (A kid's guide to drawing the presidents of the United States of America)
Includes bibliographical references and index.
ISBN 1-4042-2987-6 (Lib. Binding : alk. paper)
1. Tyler, John, 1790–1862—Juvenile literature. 2. Presidents—United States—Biography—Juvenile literature. 3. Drawing—Technique—Juvenile literature. I. Title. II. Series.

E397.Z36 2006
973.5'8—dc22
                                    2004018444

Manufactured in the United States of America

Contents

A True Leader

John Tyler was the first vice president ever to become leader of the United States following the death of a president. When William Henry Harrison died in 1841, after only a month in office, Tyler checked the Constitution and believed it said he should take over as president. Other lawmakers disagreed, but Tyler stuck to his beliefs. He set such a good example after he carried out a peaceful change in leadership that all future vice presidents would follow his lead after the deaths of presidents.

Tyler was born in Charles City County, Virginia, in 1790. His father, Judge John Tyler, was once governor of Virginia. Though his mother, Mary Armistead Tyler, died when he was seven years old, Tyler remembered having a happy childhood. When he was 12, he went to school at the College of William and Mary in Williamsburg, Virginia. He graduated in 1807, and went on to study law. He became a lawyer two years later.

Politics also interested Tyler. Between the years 1811 and 1839, Tyler was a representative in the Virginia legislature, a U.S. congressman and senator, and a governor of Virginia. Despite his being busy, Tyler found time for love. He met Letitia Christian at a party near his home and married her in 1813. They had eight children. In 1842, Letitia died after she was weakened by a stroke. Tyler had another chance at love with Julia Gardiner of New York. They married in 1844, while he was president.

You will need the following supplies to draw the life and times of John Tyler:

✓ A sketch pad   ✓ An eraser   ✓ A pencil   ✓ A ruler

These are some of the shapes and drawing terms you need to know:

Horizontal Line	——	Squiggly Line	∿
Oval	⬭	Trapezoid	⏢
Rectangle	▭	Triangle	△
Shading	▰	Vertical Line		
Slanted Line	/	Wavy Line	∿

A Life of Public Service

Tyler took the oath of office as the tenth president of the United States in 1841. To avoid more confusion in Washington D.C., Tyler kept Harrison's advisers. This led to many problems, however. Many of the advisers and several other politicians in Congress supported the leader of the Whig Party, Henry Clay, who wanted to be the next president. The Whigs, including Tyler, were a group of men who were joined in their strong dislike for the ideas and practices of Andrew Jackson and Martin Van Buren.

Not long into his presidency, all but one member of the entire cabinet quit. On top of this, the Whigs threw Tyler out of their party, hoping he would leave the presidency. Tyler held firm again. He appointed other men who were friendlier to him as advisers, and he continued to do his job. Under his command the northeastern border between the United States and Canada was settled in 1842. Tyler approved a bill to annex Texas shortly before his term ended in 1845.

John Tyler served as president from 1841 to 1845. In the years following his presidency, Tyler tried to ease the growing problems between the North and the South. His peacemaking efforts failed. Because of his belief in states' rights, he encouraged Virginia to leave the United States in 1861. Because of this he was known for a long time as a traitor to the Union.

John Tyler's Virginia

John Tyler was born in this house on Greenway Plantation.

Virginia

Map of the United States of America

The tenth president of the United States was born and raised on his family's estate, called Greenway, which lies along the James River in Charles City County, Virginia. During John Tyler's childhood, Greenway was a plantation that grew wheat, corn, and tobacco. A plantation is a very large farm. Today the government considers the estate a historic place.

Another Virginian landmark is Sherwood Forest Plantation, where Tyler retired after his presidency. The plantation also rests along the James River, fewer than 3 miles (5 km) away from Greenway. In 1845, Tyler added a 68-foot (21 m) ballroom to the house, making it more than 300 feet (91 m) long. To this day it is the longest house of its kind in the country. Tyler's grandson and his family live there today. They have opened up part of their home to the public.

When Tyler died in 1862, he was buried in Hollywood Cemetery in Richmond, Virginia. At that time many people thought he had committed treason against the Union. In 1915, Congress finally erected a monument in his honor at the grave. The structure has a bronze sculpture of Tyler and bears the seals of the United States and the state of Virginia. It was built by planners T. F. McGann & Sons Company of Boston, Massachusetts.

In this photograph you can see the grave and sculpture of John Tyler. Also buried in Hollywood Cemetery is President James Monroe, whose resting place is in the dark-domed grave in the background. Hollywood Cemetery was planned in 1847 and is one of America's most beautiful "garden" cemeteries, with plenty of paths, valleys, hills, and trees.

The Making of a President

John Tyler was born on March 29, 1790. He was one of eight children born to Judge John and Mary Armistead Tyler. Young John was known as a gentle but

stubborn boy. At 10 years old, he led a class strike against a teacher who beat students with a stick. His father did not punish him because he believed his son did the right thing.

John looked up to his father, who served in federal and state courts and as governor of Virginia from 1808 to 1811. Judge Tyler believed, as his college friend Thomas Jefferson did, that the Constitution gave the federal government only limited power over the states. Young John embraced this idea and learned more about it at the College of William and Mary, shown above, where he went to school from 1802 to 1807. While at school Tyler proved himself to be a very good violinist. He also showed an interest in subjects such as history and law.

1

You are going to draw the College of William and Mary. Draw a rectangle. Next draw a line down the center, extending beyond the rectangle as shown.

2

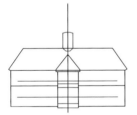

Draw the roof. Draw a horizontal line across the rectangle. Draw a small rectangle in the center. Draw a triangular roof on it. Note that the two bottom corners are flat rather than pointed.

3

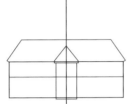

Erase any extra lines. Draw three short horizontal lines across the rectangle you drew in step 2. Draw two long horizontal lines across the main rectangle. Begin to draw the tower on the roof.

4

Erase the extra lines. Along the horizontal guides, draw the rectangles for windows. Draw six shapes on the roof for chimneys. Add lines to the top of the tower you started in step 3.

5

Erase the window guidelines. Draw slanted lines on the roof shape. Draw a horizontal line across the roof. Add lines inside the center triangle. Draw vertical lines inside the center rectangle. Add a door and a window.

6

Erase extra lines. Using the guides you added above, draw the pointed windows on the roof. Add windows and a circle to the tower. Draw windows and a circle in the center. Draw rough lines for the ground.

7

Erase the center guideline except for the pole on the roof. Erase extra lines. Look carefully at the drawing and add the lines as shown to the tower, the roof, the windows, and the entrance.

8

You can finish your drawing with shading. Well done! You did a great job.

Early Political Career

At the early age of 19, Tyler became a lawyer. He was such a great speaker that he won most of his cases. He became well known and was voted into  the Virginia legislature in 1811. He was reelected every year for the next five years.

In 1816, he was elected to the U.S. Congress and was then elected for two more terms after that. Tyler campaigned against the national bank at this time. He also fought for Missouri's right to make its own laws about slavery as it entered the Union. Tyler did not get his way on these issues. Tired and unhappy, he quit Congress in 1821.

He was voted back into the Virginia legislature two years later. In 1825, he became the governor of Virginia and was reelected the next year. As governor he supported building roads and canals, like the one shown above, between eastern and western Virginia. The construction helped improve trade and communication within the state.

1

Let's draw the boats on the canal. Start by drawing a rectangle. Draw a curving long line with short ends as shown. Add a trapezoid with an arch under it as shown.

2

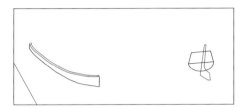

Draw a slanted line in the left corner of the rectangle. Draw the long curving lines on the first shape. Draw the rudder on the other shape as shown. The rudder steers the boat.

3

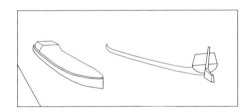

Draw the top to the boat on the left. Draw the long lines for the body of the boat on the right. Erase the lines of the boat that go through the rudder. Add lines to the rudder.

4

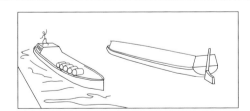

Draw the side of the right boat. Add barrels to the left boat. Draw windows at the back of the boat and a curved line at the front. Draw a stick figure. Draw squiggly lines for the water.

5

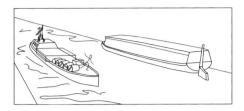

Draw slanted lines coming from the back and front of the boat on the right. Add more water lines. Draw the lines around the stick figure. Add another stick figure. Add details to both boats.

6

Draw more people. Draw the poles that the people use to push the boat. Erase extra lines. Add more barrels. Draw more squiggly water lines. Draw window lines on the right boat. Draw a stick figure on it, too.

7

Erase extra lines. Draw the outline of the stick figure you just drew. Add more people.

8

Erase extra lines. You can finish with shading. Notice where the shading is darker in some areas than others.

The National Bank

Tyler was elected twice to the U.S. Senate, beginning his first term in 1827 and his second in 1833. Throughout his political career, Tyler campaigned against the national bank, which he thought was unconstitutional. The bank was first established in 1791 to help the new Union become more financially secure. The bank closed in 1811 but reopened in 1816 to help the unstable economy. Three years later, however, the bank was in trouble because of corruption. Tyler called for the government to close the bank, but it remained open until its contract ended in 1836.

President Andrew Jackson had vetoed a bill to renew the national bank in 1832. The next year he withdrew government funds and placed them in different state banks. Many lawmakers, including Tyler, thought Jackson's act went against the Constitution and voted to condemn him publicly in 1834. When politicians friendly to Jackson pressured senators to clear Jackson's name, Tyler quit the Senate in protest.

1

Start your drawing of the national bank by drawing a rectangle. Draw lines on either side of the bottom line.

2

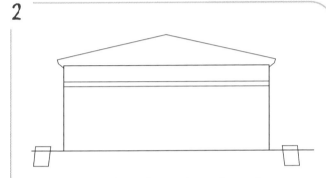

Add a pointed roof. See how the sides go beyond the edges of the rectangle. Draw two horizontal lines across the top of the rectangle. Draw two slanting shapes at the bottom, one on each side.

3

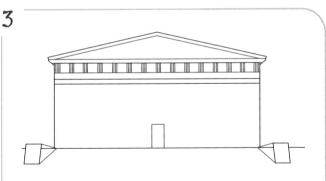

Erase the lines that go through the slanting shapes. Draw lines to form triangles next to them. Add a door. Add lines to form a triangle in the roof. The bottom line of the triangle reaches the edges of the roof. Add another horizontal line at the top of the rectangle. Draw many short vertical lines above it.

4

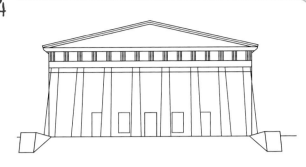

Add two more slanted lines that come to a point at the roof. Draw slanting columns. Draw two windows and two doors. Erase the lines that went through the two triangles at the bottom.

5

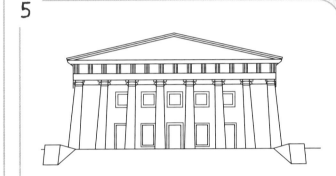

Erase extra lines in the columns. Add details to the tops of the columns. Add more windows. Draw outlines around the windows and doors.

6

Erase the extra lines at the tops of the columns. Add as much detail as you would like to your drawing. Finish with shading. Your drawing of the national bank is now complete!

Tippecanoe and Tyler Too

When Tyler left the Senate, he joined the Whigs. In 1835, the Democrats nominated Van Buren for president and Richard Johnson for vice president.

The Whigs nominated several candidates for each office, including Tyler for vice president. The Whigs lost. Van Buren and Johnson won the 1836 election.

The Whigs tried again in 1840 with just one set of candidates. They were William Harrison for president and Tyler for vice president. Using colorful songs and posters, like the one shown here, the Whigs campaigned under the slogan, "Tippecanoe and Tyler Too." Old Tippecanoe was another name for William Harrison, a major general in the army who had won a battle at Tippecanoe, Indiana. Another part of the Whig campaign was to present Harrison as a common man, just as the voters were, who drank cider and lived in a log cabin. The Whigs' campaign worked. Harrison and Tyler won and began their terms on March 4, 1841.

1

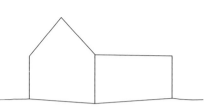

You are going to draw the log cabin from a Harrison and Tyler campaign poster. Draw a wavy line. Next draw three vertical lines. Draw a horizontal line connecting the tops of two of the vertical lines. Draw two slanted lines to make the top of a triangle.

2

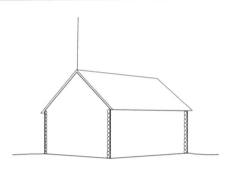

Draw the roof of the cabin. Draw a vertical line for a pole on top. Draw small ovals on the sides as shown. These will become the ends of the logs.

3

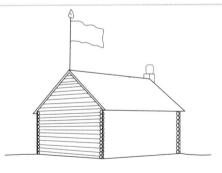

Draw wavy lines for the flag on the pole. Draw the shape at the top of the pole. Draw the shapes for the chimney. Draw lines for the logs across the side of the cabin. Draw more ovals at the sides of the cabin.

4

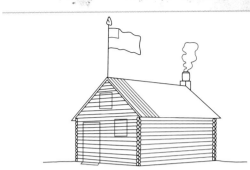

Draw lines at the corner of the flag. Draw smoke coming from the chimney. Add a line to the top of the chimney. Draw more logs on the side of the cabin. Erase extra lines. Draw two windows. Draw a door with a line at the bottom for a step. Draw some slanted lines on the roof.

5

Finish drawing the slanted lines on the roof. Draw four more lines going across the roof. Draw squiggly lines across most of the flag. Erase the lines of the logs that went through the windows and door. Add outlines for the windows and door. Draw an animal skin as shown. Draw another window.

6

Erase the lines inside the last window you drew and inside the animal skin. Add details to the flag and the window. Finish with shading.

The Accidental President

John Tyler was living in Williamsburg, Virginia, when Harrison died of pneumonia on April 4, 1841. Vice presidents at that time had few responsibilities, so Tyler had been expecting to lead a quiet life at home. When he heard about Harrison's death, he immediately went to Washington to take control as president. He met with Harrison's advisers and decided to keep them in the cabinet. The advisers said they expected Tyler to have the cabinet vote on all important decisions, as Harrison had done. Tyler refused. "I am President, and I shall be held responsible for my administration," he said firmly.

Those who were unhappy with Tyler's actions called him His Accidency, or Acting President. Tyler did not pay attention to them and only answered people who called him by his proper title. As always Tyler stood up for what he believed was right.

1 You are now going to draw the silk ribbon announcing Tyler's rise to the presidency. Begin by drawing two rectangles as shown. The smaller rectangle is very slightly off center.

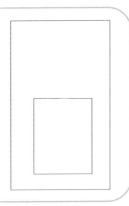

2 Draw another rectangle around the small rectangle. This is the picture frame. Draw ovals at the top of the frame for the eagle. Draw an oval and a straight line inside the frame.

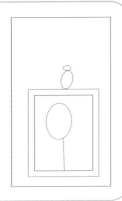

3 Draw guidelines for the eagle's wings. Draw lines for Tyler's eyes, nose, and mouth. Add a curve to the side of the oval. Add an oval for his ear. Draw lines for his neck and shoulders. Add details to the bottom right corner of the frame.

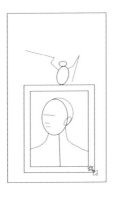

4 Write "THE PRESIDENT" in a curve across the top. Draw the eagle's neck, eye, and beak. Draw Tyler's eyes, nose, cheek, and jaw. Draw the lines inside the ear. Erase any extra lines from the frame. Add more lines and details to the frame.

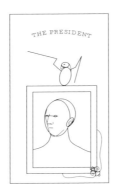

5 Add the words "OF THE." Erase extra lines on the eagle. Draw lines for wings. Draw Taylor's hair, eyebrows, and pupils. Erase the eye and nose guides, and part of the head and ear ovals. Draw his collar. Add details to the frame's side.

6 Add the words "UNITED STATES." Draw the ribbon in the eagle's beak and the line under his wing. Erase the extra lines on Tyler's head. Draw his mouth, chin, and eyelids. Draw lines for his clothing. Add details to the frame.

7 Erase any extra lines. Write "LIBERTY AND INDEPENDENCE" on the ribbon. Add lines to the wings. Add lines to Tyler's face and chest. Add all the tiny details to the picture frame as shown. Take your time.

8 Erase any extra lines. Look at the photograph and the drawing carefully and finish with shading. Well done! You are finished drawing the silk ribbon.

Henry Clay and John Tyler

During Tyler's presidency, Whig leader Henry Clay, who is shown here, presented a plan that would establish a new national bank. Congress and the Senate approved it, but Tyler used his presidential power to veto it. He believed the plan did not allow states to choose whether they wanted a national bank.

The veto made the Whigs angry, including many of Tyler's advisers. Clay tried to set aside the veto but failed. Then he presented another bank bill, which passed through Congress and the Senate. When Clay heard Tyler would veto his bill again, he said, "I will live to be a hundred years and devote them all to the extermination of Tyler and his friends!"

Hoping to make Tyler leave the White House, Clay convinced all but one of the president's advisers to quit their jobs. He also had Tyler kicked out of the Whig Party. In spite of these efforts, Tyler remained in office and appointed other men to the cabinet.

1 Start your drawing of Henry Clay by making a large oval. Draw a smaller oval inside it for Clay's head. Draw more ovals for his ears. Draw the outline of his neck and shoulders. Draw guidelines for his eyes, nose, and mouth.

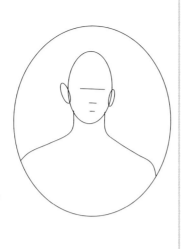

2 Draw the shapes shown for his eyes. Draw lines around the head oval for his hair. Draw the shape of his face inside the oval guideline. Draw the shape of the collar at his neck.

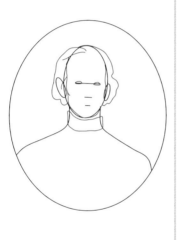

3 Erase extra lines. Draw circles in his eyes. Add a line for some more of his hair. Draw lines for his nose, chin, and mouth. Draw the bow tie and part of his shirt and jacket as shown. Don't forget the lines for his shirt collar.

4 Erase any extra lines in the bow and shirt collar. Erase the guides for the mouth and nose. Add details to the bow as shown. Draw his eyebrows and add pupils and a curve under the eye on the left. Add details to his hair and ears.

5 Add lines for his eyelids and his chin as shown. Draw lines for shoulders and the collar of his jacket. Erase the ear guide ovals.

6 Erase the shoulder outline. You can finish with shading. If you like you can use the side of your pencil tip to shade in the background. Good job.

Foreign Affairs

Even with his troubles in Washington, D.C., President Tyler was able to deal effectively with foreign affairs. Secretary of State Daniel Webster was a great help. Webster worked with Great Britain's Lord Ashburton to establish the boundary lines between Canada and the states of New York, Vermont, New Hampshire, and Maine. The Webster-Ashburton Treaty of 1842 established what is now the northeastern border of the United States.

That same year Tyler was able to answer a call for help from Prince Timoleo Haolilio of the Sandwich Islands, which are now Hawaii. The Prince feared the British or the French would take control of the land. Because the islands were near Asian markets, where the United States wanted to trade, Tyler warned the European nations to stay away. The warning worked and the Sandwich Islands were recognized as an independent nation. Shown here is a small statue that was brought back from the Sandwich Islands in the 1800s.

1

Begin by drawing a large oval. This is your guide for drawing the statue's head. Draw stick lines as shown for guides to the body. Notice how the head oval is very large compared to the body.

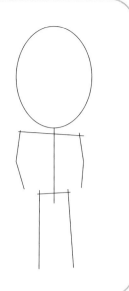

2

Draw lines for the nose as shown. Draw long curvy lines for the eye shapes. Draw the shape that looks like a dog's bone for the mouth area.

3

Erase any extra lines on the head oval. Draw another large bone shape around the mouth. Draw two curved lines inside the mouth area. Connect the eyes with a curved line. Draw wavy lines inside the eye areas. Draw a large rough curve around the top of the head oval.

4

Erase the rest of the head oval. Draw the outline of the body shape around the guidelines you drew in step 1. Draw curvy lines on the mouth as shown. Add a line across the bottom of the mouth area. Draw a squiggly line above the eyes.

5

Fill in the head shape with a lot of squiggly lines. Add more lines to the eyes. Erase the body guidelines. Add lines to the body as shown. Draw the lines for the base between the feet. Add lines to each side of the body extending from the head shape to the bottom of the arms.

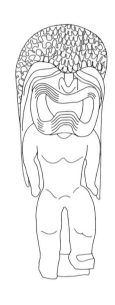

6

You can finish your drawing of the statue from the Sandwich Islands with shading. Notice where the shading is darker in some parts than in others. Well done! You are finished.

Tyler and Texas

President Tyler worked hard to annex, or add, Texas to the Union. He had a vision of the United States as a great nation, able to compete economically with Britain. He believed that Texas's rich soil would help make that dream real. He was sure this annexation would make him a memorable president.

Texas had fought for independence from Mexico in 1836. Right away the new republic had wanted to become a part of the United States, but politicians had stayed away from the offer. Annexation would bring up unwanted debates about admitting Texas as a slave state or as a free state. During that time there were already deep divisions between the North and the South regarding the issue of slavery. These differences would later lead to the Civil War. After many unsuccessful attempts to annex Texas, Tyler finally got his way. Just before he ended his term as president on March 3, 1845, Tyler signed the treaty that added Texas to the Union.

1 You are now going to draw a map of Texas and the area surrounding it. Start by drawing a rectangle. Draw a line across the rectangle and then another one down the middle. These will be your guides.

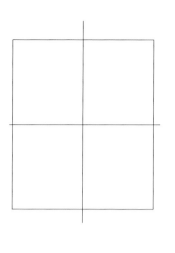

2

Let's begin by drawing squiggly lines for the outline of the map of Texas. Notice how most of it is inside the lower right rectangle, although it does cross over into the other rectangles.

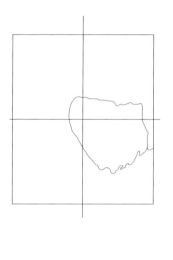

3 Draw a long squiggly line from the upper left rectangle down through the lower left rectangle and finally to the lower right rectangle. Be sure to join this line to the bottom part of Texas. The area to the left of this line is Mexico.

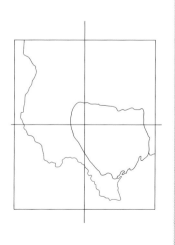

4 Draw another squiggly line going from the top left corner and joining Texas on its northern border. Draw the four squiggly lines for rivers. Draw a round shape off the coast of Texas. Add another squiggly line at the bottom.

5 Erase the guidelines. You can finish your map with shading. You can use the side of your pencil tip to lightly shade in the entire map. See the areas where the shading is slightly darker. The darkest part is the newly annexed Texas.

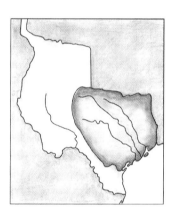

Retirement

After a lifetime of public service, Tyler was finally able to live quietly. He and his second wife, Julia, shown here,

retired to an estate called Sherwood Forest in Charles City County. Here Tyler spent time with his family and became a farmer. He also kept up with current events. The rising hostilities between the North and the South concerned him. In 1860, South Carolina withdrew from the Union, and other southern states were in danger of doing the same thing. President James Buchanan sent Tyler to a peace conference to try to find a compromise between the North and the South. Tyler soon realized war was impossible to avoid. Although he did not want to see the country fall apart, he wanted to protect his home state and states' rights. He encouraged Virginia to withdraw from the Union. He was elected to the Confederate Congress but died in 1862 before he could take his seat.

1

Draw a rectangle. Draw a vertical line down the center of the rectangle. Notice how the line extends above the top of the rectangle.

2

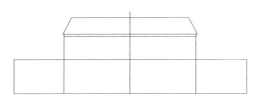

Add a roof as shown. Draw a horizontal line beneath the roof. Add a long rectangle going across the front of the building.

3

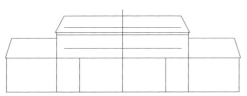

Add more lines for two roofs on each side. Draw two horizontal lines in the main part of the building. These will be guides for the windows. Draw two vertical lines. This will be the front porch.

4

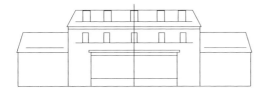

Erase parts of the horizontal lines at the sides of the porch. Draw lines on the porch. Add windows. Draw two horizontal lines on each side roof.

5

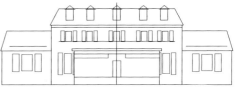

Draw more windows and add rectangles beside all the windows for shutters. Draw triangles on top of the roof windows. Erase the roof window guide. Draw two small shapes near the top of the porch. Draw a door.

6

Erase extra lines. Add shapes to the windows on the roofs. Draw two chimneys. Add more windows as shown on either side. Add details to the porch.

7

Erase extra lines. Draw lines at the sides of the chimneys. Add tiny ovals to the top of the porch. Add slanted lines that cross over each other to the porch. Draw short vertical lines in the porch area, too. Draw two horizontal lines across the bottom of the building.

8

Erase the center guideline. Add as much detail as you would like. Finish your drawing of Sherwood Forest with shading.

The Legacy of John Tyler

Tyler was a true supporter of the Constitution. Because he stood up for his right to lead, he made it easier for future vice presidents to take control after the deaths of Presidents Zachary Taylor, Abraham Lincoln, James Garfield, William McKinley, Warren  Harding, Franklin Roosevelt, and John F. Kennedy.

Tyler also preserved the balance of power between the presidency and Congress. When the Whigs tried to force him to quit, he held his ground. He said if he gave up, it would show the world that "our system of government had failed."

Tyler was also a visionary and saw the United States as a future world leader. Under his command the Union improved relations with Britain and China, acquired Texas, and came one step closer to securing Hawaii. Although Tyler was unpopular at the time of his death because of his allegiance to the South, his record shows he was a true public servant to the Union.

1

Begin your drawing of John Tyler by drawing a rectangle. Draw an oval that tilts slightly to the left for the head. Draw a long line coming from the oval. This will be your guideline for the neck and body.

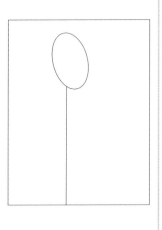

2

Add a curved line for the back of the head. Add an oval for the ear. Draw horizontal guidelines for the eyes, nose, and mouth. Draw guidelines for the shoulders, arms, and hand as shown.

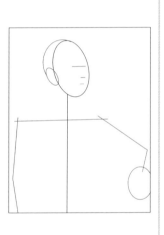

3

Draw lines for the ear, eye, eyebrows, and nose as shown. Draw a basic outline for the body around the guidelines you drew in the last step.

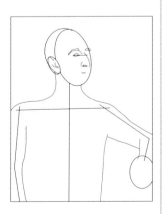

4

Erase the body, ear, and nose guides. Add lines to the eye you drew in step 3. Add his other eye. Draw his mouth, chin, and cheek. Draw his hair and add details to his ear. Draw the lines for Tyler's jacket. Draw his fingers. Draw the paper that he holds.

5

Erase extra lines on the head. Add details to his face and hair. Add lines for his clothes. Don't forget to draw the button on his shirt! Draw the small part of the chair that is between his body and his arm on the right side of the drawing.

6

You can now erase the body outline. Finish your drawing with shading. You can use the side of your pencil tip to shade in the background. Notice how dark his jacket is compared to the rest of the drawing. Well done!

Timeline

1790 John Tyler is born.

1811 Tyler is elected to the Virginia legislature and is reelected every year for the next five years.

1813 John Tyler and Letitia Christian are married.

1816 Tyler is chosen to fill an opening in the U.S. Congress.

1821 Missouri is admitted to the Union as a slave state. Tyler quits Congress.

1823 Tyler is reelected to the Virginia legislature.

1825 Tyler becomes governor of Virginia and is reelected the next year.

1827 Tyler takes office as U.S. senator and is reelected after the first term.

1836 Tyler leaves the Senate and becomes a Whig.

1838 Tyler is reelected to the Virginia legislature.

1841 John Tyler becomes vice president but soon becomes president when William Henry Harrison dies.

1842 Letitia Tyler dies in the White House.

1842 The Webster-Ashburton Treaty establishes the northeastern boundary of the United States.

1844 Tyler marries Julia Gardiner. The United States signs a treaty with China.

1845 Tyler signs a bill to bring Texas into the Union.

1861 The Civil War begins.

1862 Tyler dies before meeting with the Confederate Congress.

1915 Congress honors Tyler with a monument at Hollywood Cemetery in Virginia.

Glossary

administration (ad-mih-nuh-STRAY-shun) A group of people in charge of something.

allegiance (uh-LEE-jents) Support of a country, group, or cause.

annex (A-neks) To take over or add to.

cabinet (KAB-nit) A group of people who act as advisers to government officials.

communication (kuh-myoo-nih-KAY-shun) The sharing of facts or feelings.

compromise (KOM-pruh-myz) To give up something to reach an agreement.

Congress (KON-gres) The part of the U.S. government that makes laws.

Constitution (kon-stih-TOO-shun) The basic rules by which the United States is governed.

corruption (kuh-RUP-shun) Dishonesty.

devote (dih-VOHT) To give effort, attention, and time to a purpose.

extermination (ik-ster-meh-NAY-shun) Destruction.

extraordinary (ik-STROR-duh-ner-ee) Unusual or remarkable.

foreign (FOR-in) Outside one's own country.

future (FYOO-chur) The time that is coming.

landmark (LAND-mark) A building, structure, or place that is worthy of notice.

lawyer (LOY-er) Person who gives advice about the law.

legislature (LEH-jis-lay-chur) A body of people that can make or pass laws.

nominated (NAH-mih-nayt-ed) Suggested that someone or something should be given an award or a position.

oath (OHTH) A promise.

pneumonia (noo-MOHN-ya) An illness that people can get in their lungs.

slogan (SLOH-gin) A word or phrase used in politics or advertising to sell an idea.

stubborn (STUH-burn) Wanting to have one's own way.

unconstitutional (un-kon-stih-TOO-shuh-nul) Having to do with going against the basic rules by which a country or a state is governed.

vetoed (VEE-tohd) To not allow laws proposed by another branch of government to pass.

visionary (VIH-zhuh-ner-ee) A person who dreams.

Index

Web Sites

Due to the changing nature of Internet links, PowerKids Press has developed an online list of Web sites related to the subject of this book. This site is updated regularly. Please use this link to access the list:
www.powerkidslinks.com/kgdpusa/tyler/